Facts About the Arctic Hare

By Lisa Strattin

# Facts for Kids Picture Books by Lisa Strattin

Ladybugs and Fireflies, Vol 1

Squids Will Be Squids, Vol 2

Manx Cats, Vol 3

Chipmunks, Vol 5

Hummingbirds, Vol 7

African Elephants, Vol 8

American Alligators, Vol 9

Anaconda, Vol 11

Blue and Gold Macaw, Vol 13

Burrowing Owl, Vol 18

Sign Up for New Release Emails Here

http://LisaStrattin.com/subscribe-here

Monthly Surprise Box

http://KidCraftsByLisa.com

3

Contents

# INTRODUCTION

The Arctic Hare which is also called the Polar Rabbit, is a rabbit family which has evolved and adapted to the harsh wintery conditions in the arctic regions and other mountainous, snowy areas.

It is hard to survive such harsh winters, but these rabbits have a thick coat of fur to keep them warm.

Since the snow cover also serves as a very good insulator, they burrow holes in the ground to keep themselves away from the cold winds and snow storms.

## CHARACTERISTICS

These Arctic Hares have a habit of being solitary, roaming around and searching for food all alone. Sometimes, they are found with a partner.

Whenever they have to change their home due to a lack of available food, they will travel with many arctic hares, sometimes as many as a dozen. This rabbit is so fast that it can cover as many as 35 miles in just one hour.

## APPEARANCE

In simple terms, anything that looks like a Rabbit in the cold snowy areas with a white thick fur coat, is the Arctic Hare. The length of the rabbit's ears is significantly shorter than other rabbits you might see, which makes them easy to identify.

## LIFE STAGES

This species of rabbit mates between the months of May and April each year. The female has its babies between late May and the end of July. They do move to the northernmost part of their habitat when it is time to have their babies. She delivers them in a nest she has burrowed into the ground. There are usually around eight babies in a litter. After they are born, the mother stays for only a few days. After that, the young ones remain still and quiet so that predators will not find them.

## LIFE SPAN

There has not been a lot of study of the life span of the Arctic Hares. But the information collected to-date has shown that in the raw wild conditions, these rabbits have the ability to live for 3 to 5 years.

The do not seem to live well in captivity because it is difficult to keep the temperatures cold enough for them to thrive. For this reason, the average life span of these animals in captive conditions is only one to one and a half years.

## SIZE

The average length of the rabbit is 15 to 28 inches. However, this measurement does not count their tail, which in itself is 2 to 4 inches long.

They weigh between 5 to 12 pounds. There have been some found that weigh 15 pounds, but this is an exceptionally large Arctic Hare.

18

## HABITAT

The Arctic Hare lives only in the arctic areas of the world including cold deserts and mountain ranges. Since it is a leaf-eating rabbit, it prefers the mountains because there is a variety of food found there. It lives from Greenland's northernmost regions and ranges, the arctic islands of the Caribbean to the northern parts of Canada.

## DIET

The rabbits eat mostly leaves, so it needs to live in areas where there are plenty of them around. If the food supply grows scarce, the Arctic Hares just moves to a better place with more food. Besides leaves, they will also eat things that thrive on plants and wood, like mosses, some twigs. seaweed and blossoms.

## FRIENDS AND ENEMIES

The Arctic Hares do not do not like to be in social groups with other hares.

Their enemies are the Arctic Fox, the Grey Wolf, Ermine and the Rough-Legged Hawk.

## SUITABILITY AS PETS

Hares have always been good pets for people. The biggest problem with the Arctic Hare as a pet is keeping the cold temperatures for their habitat.

It is very difficult to keep one of these rabbits as a pet, so you would be better off choosing a rabbit that is readily available at your local pet store.

# COLOR ME

# COLOR ME

# COLOR ME

**Please leave me a review here:**

*http://lisastrattin.com/Review-Vol-65*

**For more Kindle Downloads Visit Lisa Strattin Author Page on Amazon Author Central**

*http://amazon.com/author/lisastrattin*

**To see upcoming titles, visit my website at LisaStrattin.com– all books available on kindle!**

*http://lisastrattin.com*

You can get one by copying and pasting this link into your browser:

**http://lisastrattin.com/plusharctichare**

## MONTHLY SURPRISE BOX

**Get yours by copying and pasting this link into your browser**

**http://KidCraftsByLisa.com**

Made in the USA
Monee, IL
20 February 2020